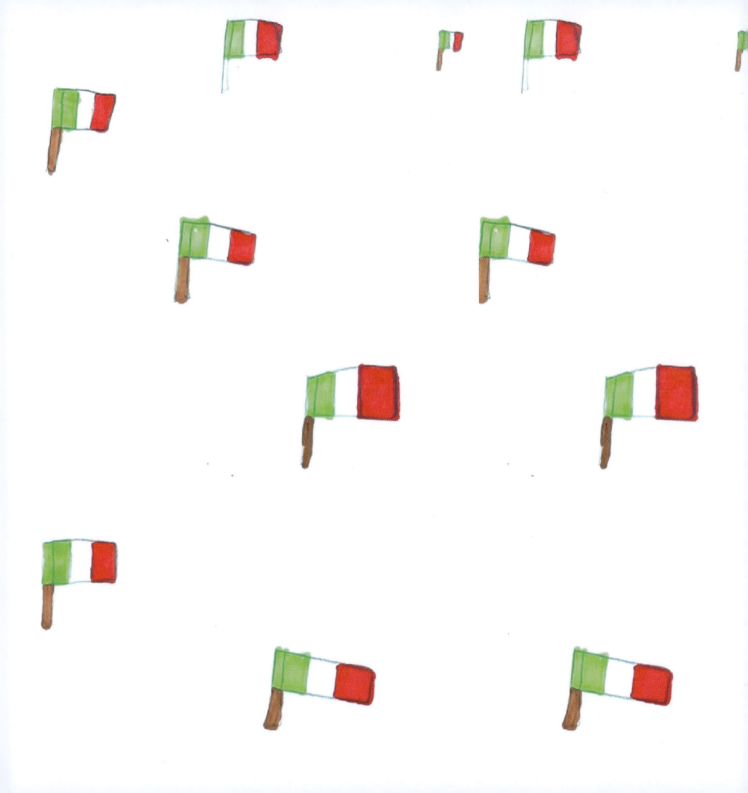

Acknowledgements

I would like to say thanks to my Mummy, who encouraged me to create this book.

I went to Italy on holiday in the summer of 2022. Thanks to my parents who booked such a great adventure, the inspiration behind this book.

Happy reading,
Jasmine

Foreword

Take a tour with Rose to visit the beautiful sights of Italy and learn a fact about each one. It may tempt you to find out more. Maybe you will visit Italy one day and have a fun fact to tell someone.

Jasmine has beautifully captured in her drawings and her words, the delights that Italy has to offer!

Rachel Brand.

Travel through Italy with Rose....

Author and Illustrator
Jasmine Paver

On the first day of her holiday, Rose visited Venice.

Did you know instead of roads Venice has canals?

Rather than travelling by car, travel is by gondolas.

Can you spot the gondola in the picture?

On the second day, Rose visited the Trevi Fountain in Rome.

According to the legend, if you throw a coin over your shoulder into the fountain, you will return back to Rome.

Did you know that the flowing water is recycled and there is no waste?

On the third day, while in Rome, Rose visited the Colosseum.

Did you know that the Colosseum is the world's largest amphitheatre?

Coffee served with chocolate

On the fourth day, Rose went to a coffee shop with her family. There are coffee shops all over Italy, some coffees are served with a chocolate or a biscuit.

Did you know that most people in Italy prefer coffee to most other drinks?

What is your favourite chocolate?

Can you spot the chocolate spoon?

Leaning Tower of Pisa

On the sixth day, Rose visited the Leaning Tower of Pisa.

It is leaning to one side and located in the city of Pisa, which is why it is called the 'Leaning Tower of Pisa'.

In the picture on the left, can you find the two people walking?

On the eighth day,
Rose visited a gelato shop and enjoyed the delicious mango flavoured ice cream.

Did you know in Italy, they sell gelato flavours such as banana, melon, coconut, apple, fig and orange.

What is your favourite ice cream flavour?

On the ninth day, Rose visited the Cinque Terre region. This region is made up of 5 different villages.

Did you know that Cinque means five in Italian?

Count with me to ten in Italian - uno, due, tre, quattro, cinque, sei, sette, otto, nove and dieci.

On the tenth day,
Rose visited the Amalfi Coast.

Rose snorkelled in the deep, blue sea off the Amalfi coast. The sea water was warm and clear.

Snorkelling is great fun as you may see colourful fish swimming around in the sea.

Would you like to snorkel in the sea?

On the eleventh day, the last day of her holiday, Rose went on a boat to the Capri Island, past the Faraglioni rocks.

Did you know that Capri Island is also known as the Island of the Mermaids.

Have you ever jumped in the waves? Which is your favourite beach?

Rose loved her adventure in Italy!

She is looking forward to her next adventure and , one day, would love to share it with you....

Some facts about Italy

Flag of Italy -

Capital of Italy - **Rome**

National sport of Italy - **Football**

Currency in Italy - **Euro**

<u>About the author</u>

My name is Jasmine Paver. I am 11 years old.

I live in Bristol with my parents and my twin brother.

I love playing netball and reading books. One of my hobbies is creating artwork using different mediums.

I hope you enjoyed reading this book!

This is me admiring an artwork in one of the Italian art galleries.

Thanks for buying and reading my book,
Jasmine ♡

Printed in Great Britain
by Amazon